How a Gray Seed Became a Peace Lily

Karen Raffa

How A Gray Seed Became A Peace Lily
Copyright © 2024 by Karen Raffa

Published in the United States of America
ISBN   Paperback: 979-8-89091-479-8
ISBN   eBook: 979-8-89091-480-4

All rights reserved. No part of this publication may be reproduced, stored in a retrieval system or transmitted in any way by any means, electronic, mechanical, photocopy, recording or otherwise without the prior permission of the author except as provided by USA copyright law.

The opinions expressed by the author are not necessarily those of ReadersMagnet, LLC.

ReadersMagnet, LLC
10620 Treena Street, Suite 230 | San Diego, California, 92131 USA
1.619. 354. 2643 | www.readersmagnet.com

Book design copyright © 2024 by ReadersMagnet, LLC. All rights reserved.

Cover design by Ericka Obando
Interior design by Don De Guzman

Contents

Acknowledgments v
Introduction vii
My Life Shattered 1
Funeral Arrangements 6
Back to Reality 12
Thinking of the Future 25
Spiritual Awakening 30
Spiritual Growth 34
Choosing Joy 38
Season of Contentment 41
My Lasting Message of Hope 43
About the Author 45
Epilogue 47

Acknowledgments

First and foremost, I thank God through Jesus Christ and the Holy Spirit for rescuing me from certain death and giving me the courage and strength to write this book. This is my testimony as to the healing power of God.

I dedicate this book to Shirl and my family for being a great part of my life. For many years, Shirl and I joked about writing a book about all the family drama in our lives, but I never dreamed I would actually have the patience or dedication to put pen to paper—or rather, fingers to a computer keyboard—to tell my story.

I give all thanks to God as I am no typist so it was hen and peck all the way through. It has taken me eight months to finally complete it.

I would also like to thank the people mentioned in my story as well as some that were not named though they all played an important part during my journey of healing. I have a special thanks for two people. Kathy for her compassion and understanding and Chris my secret critic who gave me her honest feedback and encouragement while writing this book. May God Bless you all.

Introduction

This book is about regaining life and purpose after devastating personal losses. I had five family members—my mom; two sisters; a niece; and Shirl, my spouse of thirty-one years—all pass away within a three-year period. Though I felt a deep loss for all, I was at peace with the passing of my mom, sisters, and niece. On the other hand, the loss of Shirl was the most devastating. This story specifically relates to the loss of my spouse, though my other family members are mentioned throughout the story.

I am no writer but I felt the need to tell my story. It is intended for anyone who has had the pain of loss so deep that only someone who's been there could understand. My story tells of the anguish I went through with my grief and then to my path of healing. It is very intense as I put my deepest, darkest feelings on paper, and there are many twists and turns. Through my journey, I learned you have to be truthful with yourself and turn to God to for true healing.

My hope is that even if one person reads and relates to my story, it was worth the pain I went through while writing it. I have also learned you have to dig deep into your soul to find your purpose in life. I found out there is meaningful life after loss, but the only real, long-lasting way of finding true inner peace and joy is through *Jesus Christ*. Praise be to God. I hope that anyone who reads it will find inspiration because life is precious and worth living for. I also hope that it encourages all to start a long-lasting personal and intimate relationship with Jesus. Thanks to all of you. *May God bless you*!

My Life Shattered

August 7, 2016, was the day that shattered my world and brought me to my knees. At noon that day, the person I loved most in this life who I had been with for thirty-one years passed away before my very eyes. It all started one month earlier.

On July fifth, we were told she has stage 4 lung cancer, which had spread to other parts of her body. The news was devastating, but I think we both thought that it would get better. You know the denial effect kicked in. There were few options (chemo and radiation). Over the next ten days, Shirl had radiation treatments. I had to work but I went to the hospital three times a day while she received radiation. After all that, she was still deteriorating. The oncologist was hesitant to start chemotherapy due to her weakened state, but I pleaded with for hours to try anyway as there was no other chance. The doctor finally agreed. Shirl had the first round on a Monday morning around eleven. About five hours later, she was looking and feeling better. She was sitting up and talking to me. They brought her a little food and she tried to eat. When they brought her back to her room, she started slipping.

In the next two days, she couldn't eat or talk much. She just laid there, moaning. It was the most painful thing to watch the person I love fading away in front of me and there was nothing I could do to help her. Then the hospital administrator and I discussed the next steps regarding her treatments. I was told Shirl would have to go to a rehab center or nursing home. Then she could come back for treatments if or when she was able to continue the chemo. About this time, a hospice got involved. They asked me if I wanted to take her home. I was floored and told them I didn't know that we had that option. I think I yelled, "Yes, I want her home!"

I had to contact work to see how much vacation I had to care for her at home. I was informed that I could use my long-term leave instead of vacation time, which I had built up to 336 hours. This was a great relief. After I filled out the paperwork, I no longer had that immediate worry of how I could be with her and get paid. Now I figured in my mind, I will get her home and make her well. Wrong! I made arrangements on Wednesday August 3rd to transport her home on Friday, August 5th. After my meeting with the staff, I went to Shirl and told her she was coming home Friday so I wouldn't see her Thursday as I had to get the room ready for her return. As I explained everything to her about coming home, she replied, "Yeah, right," and turned away from me. I said again, "You are coming home, I promise." I gave her a kiss and told her I would see her Friday. I left the room in tears from what she said. You see, these were the last words she ever said to me. Though I cried all the way home, I knew she didn't mean what she said. I had a lot to get ready with no one to help me. So with no sleep, I got everything done by Friday morning. I called her sister and brother to tell them she was coming home. They were more than welcome to visit on Saturday. Shirl arrived home at six on Friday evening. The medical staff got her all set up in the bed. All the while, she just moaned. When they left, I was relieved because I thought I could make her well now. Wrong again! See, I had put her bed where she could see Alex, her African grey parrot, and me. I talked to her constantly, reassuring her she was home, telling her how much I loved her, and telling Alex that his mommy's home. All she did was moan. I knew she must be in pain.

Within an hour of her coming home, the hospice people arrived. The nurse went over what and when to give the meds. She also explained the procedure if there were medical issues regarding her care. I had to sign a paper stating that the hospice was not an ambulance to be called if I needed help. After going over everything, Shirl was still moaning and restless in the bed. The nurse gave her some medication for pain then told me the dose needs to be given every four hours. I also need to get her some water to keep her from dehydrating as the medicine caused extreme dry mouth. I couldn't get any fluids in as it would run down her chin. Well, I came up with the idea to soak a swab in water then put in her mouth. She would bite the swab, which made me jump. I told her she scared me and then I would laugh as I gave it to her. Fifteen minutes later, she was sleeping. I was emotionally and physically exhausted. I put the birds to bed, dimmed the lights, sat in a chair across the room, and sobbed while I watched her sleep for about an hour. I decided to try and get some sleep. I set up a cot next to the bed so I could hear her if she woke up in pain. Three hours later, she started moaning again. So I followed the directions and gave her the next dose. Again, she stopped moaning in about fifteen minutes. I got up early and proceeded to feed our animals: three cats, two parrots, and four finches. I cleaned up and made coffee. I finished everything in about two hours. At this point, Shirl started moaning again. I gave her another dose.

Sometime during the day, Joan, her sister, arrived. She spent some time at Shirl's side, talking to her. Joan stayed about an hour and asked to come on Sunday. I said yes, then she left. A little while later, Walt, her brother, came and again spent time at her bedside. He was also going to come on Sunday. All throughout Saturday, I gave her the medicine, pleading with her to please wake up. She didn't. I could not understand why she wasn't waking up for me. I expected that my love and care would make her well. Things went from bad to worse as the doses I was giving her weren't working. By early evening, she was moaning louder than she had been before. I went into a panic. I called the hospice for help. I was told to increase doses to every hour. I yelled at the nurse, saying that I was killing her with the meds. The nurse kept reassuring me that I was only easing her pain and keeping her comfortable. I gave her doses every hour for about four hours. All that kept running through my mind was I was killing her since I was the one giving her the medicine. It was then and there that I knew she would never wake up. Later that night, I held her tightly. I told Shirl she needed to let go and go home to God. I told her not to try to hang on for me, that I would be okay once I knew she was no longer suffering. I held on tight and told her I would love her forever and will see her in heaven. I sobbed and held her for what seemed like hours.

I finally left the room and watched her from across the room. I didn't sleep at all that night. On Sunday, I did my chores and continued to give her medicine. I decided to give her a bath later that day. I was sitting at the table, having coffee and waiting to give her the next dose so I could wash her up. Suddenly, I looked over at her. Something didn't look or feel right. Out of intuition, I ran to the bed and checked for a pulse. There was none. I then put my ear on her chest to check for a heartbeat. Again, there was none. The person I loved most, my soulmate, just passed away in front of me. I grabbed her and began wailing, which was heard even by neighbors who told me much later. I then started reciting the Lord's Prayer. I think I said it twice before yelling, "Oh my God! Oh my God!" For a split second, I stood there not knowing what to do. At that moment, I looked at the clock. It was twelve o'clock.

Then I remembered our wedding song. I went to the stereo, punched in the CD number to the song, "I Swear" by Michael Montgomery. I cranked the volume up, which was also heard by all the neighbors, and ran back to her. I sang the song at the top of my lungs while I held her in my arms, sobbing. I played the song at least three times. I then sat down at the table and continued to sob. If have ever sobbed in pain, you know it is the deepest emotion you can ever feel. My world, as I knew it, was over. I went numb. I got on the phone and called the hospice to inform the on-call nurse that Shirl had passed away and to ask what I was supposed to do. The nurse said she would contact the funeral home and asked me how much time I wanted to wait before they would pick Shirl up. I didn't know I could keep her for a while. We agreed on two hours. The nurse said she would come over in about an hour so we could talk then.

Just then, I remembered Joan was coming over. I called her. She was already on her way I told her Shirl was gone. She was fifteen minutes away. Joan arrived a few minutes before the hospice people came. She said a prayer and gave Shirl a kiss. Joan then told me she had bought a large body pillow for Shirl, if I wanted it. I said, "Yes, thank you." Though I didn't know what I would do with it, I took the pillow over to Shirl and laid it on her then I laid on top and squeezed them as I sobbed. The pillow became very significant to me, which will become apparent later. Joan left saying that she would be in touch.

The hospice nurse came. We went over the final paperwork. She then said Shirl needed to be prepared for transport. We proceeded to remove all the catheters. Shirl was in the hospital gown so the nurse asked me if there was an item of clothing I wanted to dress her in. The first thing that came to mind was my housecoat that Shirl had bought me so we put it on her. I hugged her and kissed her again. Shortly after, the funeral staff arrived. They moved her to a gurney and started out the door. I stopped them and a told her again how much I loved her. Then she was gone. The hospice nurse sat down, trying to console me. She then told me that Carrie, their grief counselor, would be calling to check on me and would be available for a year. I asked her to thank everyone involved with Shirl's care and for supporting me. Then she left.

I was now alone, very alone. I just sat at the table and sobbed. I guess a couple hours went by. Looking at the time, I realized I had to feed our animals. I got up and did all I had to do. Then I collapsed in the chair, sobbing again. At this point, I had to spread the horrific news of Shirl's passing. I was so numb, I don't even remember who I called. But it was a short list as our circle of family and friends was very small. After all that, I called the human resources department at work to inform them of Shirl's death. Now, mind you, I was transferring from LTD paid leave for Shirl's care to going out on bereavement only five days.

I went into a panic. I called my psychiatrist to tell him of Shirl's death and to make an appointment, though I was already scheduled at a later date. You see, I was diagnosed with bipolar disorder with chronic depression twenty-eight years ago and have been in therapy for twenty-five years. I knew there was no way I would be able to go back after only five days. It was too short a time. While on the phone with HR, I was told I could stay out on long-term disability if I got a doctor's note. I told HR representative I had already contacted my psychiatrist for help. Once I got off the phone, I sat and cried. The pain in my heart was so excruciating. I literally felt that my heart was being ripped from my chest. I don't remember the next forty-eight hours except for feeding the animals and sobbing. I then started to realize I now had to make funeral arrangement and figure out how I was going to save my house. Shirl had little life insurance due to her chronic disabilities.

Funeral Arrangements

Tuesday, August 9th, I called the funeral home to make the arrangements for burial. We set for eleven on Friday morning. Now I had to go purchase our plots. We had discussed long before where we were going to be buried. We agreed on the cemetery by the Nashawannuck Pond since one of our passion was fishing. So it was only fitting for her to be near the water. I went to buy the plots. I picked the location and paid for them. After we finished, the attendant told me once I picked the date for burial, I just have the funeral home call two to three days before service so the grave can be ready. I said thank you and left. Now I had to prepare myself to meet with the funeral director to go over the process and the cost. Total at that time was $2,750.00 and did not include the urn, burial, or marker, which would be an additional $1,450. We then discussed the date for the service. I had been thinking about a date for a few days. I decided on Saturday, October 30, 2016. This was a very important date as it was our first date and kiss. Now it would be our last.

I left there knowing that now I had to contact the life insurance company and Social Security to inform them of her passing. After I took care of the insurance company and called Social Security, I was concerned that I would have to return that month's check. To my relief, I was able to keep it. Next, I had to tackle the finances as I had the funeral expenses, our regular bills, and now a 35-percent loss of income ($1,400 a month). I had to see if bills were current and when the next payments were due. Shirl always took care of the bills so I had no idea what or when to pay them. I rolled up my sleeves and started with the checking account and bills. The only good news at this point was Shirl had everything up to date. I started figuring the monthly bills and started crying. I couldn't see how I was going to pay everything or save the house. We had two car payments along with a mortgage and the rest of the bills. I just threw my hands up and sat in the chair, sobbing. After about an hour, I gathered my thoughts. I couldn't lose the house as this was our home and Shirl died here. So I started contacting creditors and started saving every penny. I only bought the bare necessities, food for the animals. I lived on sandwiches—peanut butter and jelly, tuna, and occasionally egg salad—which was okay because I didn't care about myself anyway. I was able to make temporary arrangements with creditors.

Now mind you, throughout all this stuff, I was dealing with a sinking feeling of despair plus my health (bipolar) condition was worsening. I went to the doctor for help. He wanted to know if I was suicidal. I lied to him at that time as I couldn't afford to be hospitalized with everything I was dealing with. He increased the visits to weekly. I usually saw him four times a year. Now this put more strain on my finances but I knew I had to go as I needed to survive long enough to get Shirl buried. Every day at every opportunity, I wept uncontrollably. I had no personal support network at this time. Each day I woke up expecting Shirl to be there and when she wasn't, I got upset that I was still alive and nothing had changed. I kept walking around the house looking for her, but she wasn't anywhere in the house. I guess I thought she would come out from somewhere and start talking as if the last days were all a nightmare. Wrong! The nightmare just continued.

It was 4:30 a.m. on a Sunday morning, one week to the day she passed. I was sitting at the table having coffee, which was the mainstay of my diet. While sobbing as usual, for some reason, I went looking for Shirl's favorite shirt. I found it on a chair and grabbed it. I could still smell her scent on it. I then took it, wrapped it around that body pillow, hugged it. I placed the pillow on the bed and put the blanket on her. I sat down and began sobbing. From the living room, you can see our bed as the room is totally open. A little while later, I got the birds up and fed them. While I was doing the dishes, I could hear Alex, her bird, talking, though I couldn't make out what he was saying. As I shut the water off, he said very loudly, "Karen, take a break. Have a cigarette now!" I was in shock because we never spoke like that. It had to be Shirl. I went in the room and cried. About 11:30 a.m., while I was having a cigarette and not knowing what to do, I had a thought. It was 11:58 a.m. I turned the CD to our song ("I Swear"). Then I paused it, went to the bed, and grabbed the body pillow. I turned the song on and danced with her. I sobbed and sang at the top of my lungs. After it was over, I made a commitment in that moment that I would dance with her every Sunday at noon, the time she died.

I continued to try to feel her presence in everything I did and everywhere I went. I then went looking for pictures of her so I could put them in all our rooms. I couldn't find any. I tore every room apart and found two. I got very upset as I headed to the basement, tearing through everything. I found a few more. It was then I realized most pictures we took were of our animals and not us. I ended up finding about a dozen pictures. I put some in all strategic areas so I could acknowledge her when I went in each room. This made me feel closer to her. I then found a wooden frame that had six different pictures. I remembered she was very proud that she had gotten this as a gift for me many years earlier. I took the frame and put it on my night stand next to the bed. Every night, I talked to her before bed. I told her how much I missed her and loved her. I cried uncontrollably as I wanted to be with her. I didn't want to live without her as the pain was unbearable. I kept saying I was supposed to go first. Before I shut off the light, I would say, "I love you and good night, honey, wherever you are."

I constantly looked for signs of her presence. During the week, I looked for cardinals, coins, anything that would make me feel she was with me. I started pacing around the house and staring at our houseplants, which she loved. They were starting to bloom: one gardenia, four oxalis, Christmas cactus, and even the prayer plant (also called rabbit tracks). There were many blooms. Unbelievable! Alex continued to say things that were different. Whenever I left the room, he would say, "Mommy's home!" I would run into the room, saying, "Where's your mommy? Is she here? Tell her we love her." Then he would laugh. It continues to this day. I developed a deep need to talk to her. I reached out to France (co-worker) who I knew was an animal whisperer. I asked her if she knew of any psychic I could go to for a reading. She knew a person in New Jersey. I asked if she could see if I could get a reading. I received a call that week. As we made an arrangement for a date and time, she picked September 7th at six. Mind you, she knew nothing of my situation but she picked exactly one month to the day Shirl died. When I got off the phone, I was floored and broke down again. I now had to get back to the business of getting my finances organized.

Over the next two weeks, I went to therapy, trying to get my condition stable. I already decided to commit suicide but I was waiting to get Shirl buried, change my will and insurance policy, leaving everything to the person I selected—Paul, my niece's ex-husband. I chose him because he is a warm soul and he agreed to take care of Alex, who liked him. While I was getting everything set in place, I got a call from the funeral home that Shirl's remains were back so we could finalize the burial arrangements. I met with him and told him I had chosen Saturday, October 30th for the service. Then I found out the town does not dig on the weekends. I was devastated as I was absolutely focused on that date. Now what was I going to do? I was still deteriorating and didn't care about anything. I still wanted to die but I knew I had to get Shirl buried before I could end my life. This was, I believe, my first intervention from God. See, I couldn't trust anyone to take care of Shirl's remains. So now I had to change my focus. I had to live till October 30, 2017. It had to be the date. So I took Shirl home and set her urn on a table right next to our bed. I put a picture in front of it. That is where she stayed.

With the arrangements made, I called her brother and sister to tell them the service would be next year, giving them the date and time. I continued trying to survive, going to therapy, working on the finances, and caring for my animals. Now almost a month had passed, I still cried almost continuously. I received call from Cary from the hospice. She wanted to meet with me. I met with her and we talked about Shirl's life and death. Cary asked how I as doing. I told her I couldn't get past the fact that I had killed her as I was the one giving her the drugs. She assured me that the drugs did not kill her, only relieved her pain and kept her comfortable. She asked about the type of person Shirl was. I told her she had a great sense of humor and loved animals. We had thirty-three animals in the thirty-one years we spent together. She loved the Red Sox, fishing, bingo, music, and just being together at our home. She was very giving person who always put me first but also kept me grounded. She took care of everything at home while I worked. After we met, I felt a little better but it didn't change my mind about her death. Cary continued to keep in contact. I kept in contact with the few people I had in my life. I spoke to my neighbors/friends Carolyn and Kathy often who offered their support as they knew Shirl well.

Kathy and I spoke almost daily as we both had grief issues we were dealing with. I also kept in contact with France (coworker). I was invited to her house and became friends with her and her spouse Franni. During a visit France did some animal readings for me to check on how my pets were handling Shirl's passing. I had to work with their grief and depression as well as my own. The cats (Lil Bit, seventeen years old; Abigail, eighteen; and Sparky, nineteen), our parrots (Ember, twenty-one, and Alex, six)—I tried to comfort them all by trying to avoid crying all the time in their presence.

I was so overwhelmed with everything. I had to figure out how to reduce the bills. I started figuring what bills I could get rid of. First to go was Sirius radio in her car, Schwan's Food Service, and cable TV service. Now I had two cars payments so one had to go. But which one? I tabled that decision till after I got rid of everything else I could. I minimized the electric bill by unplugging every appliance with clocks, including the stove. I put LED night light bulbs in all areas. I kept the main lights off. I used a flashlight most of the time (still do). I only used the microwave to cook for the birds and kept it unplugged. I stayed home most of the time to save on gas. I made all my trips count. I had all bills but one taken care of. I still had Discover card that I could not pay. I spent hours on the phone with them, trying to get help but they had no hardship plans. I kept paying them forty dollars per month even though it was not enough. I took every call and went over my situation to exhaustion with no results. I kept going to my doctor, trying to stabilize my mental illness. I was still in a dangerous phase. I continued to function but it was very hard as

I still wanted to end my life because I felt there was no purpose for my life anymore. Shirl was my life and many of my family members which were close to me were also gone.

Back to Reality

September 5, 2016, was my first day back to work. Oh, boy! I work for a nonprofit housing agency as a section 8 housing inspector. I woke up at four in the morning, crying as usual. I proceeded to get dressed, make coffee, feed the cats and fish, and clean the litter. Now I only had to get the birds up. I let them sleep till five thirty, which would now be two hours earlier than they were used to. I had to take care of them before I left for work and no one would be with them all day. I sat in the den with my coffee, thinking about how I was going to gather the strength to go to work and keep my emotions in check so no one would know I was dying inside. I took care of the birds then walked all throughout the house, making sure everything was okay before I left for work.

At the office, I'm always the first one there. I took a deep breath and went in. I checked my schedule (inspections) I had for that day. It was packed. I started crying. Luckily, it was still early so no one else was in. I went back to my car for a cigarette. The music on the radio was terrible. I remembered I had to disconnect Sirius radio to save money. As I was scanning stations, I heard a song that devastated me. It was called, "Tell Your Heart to Beat Again." I locked in the station only to find out it was a contemporary Christian station called K-LOVE. Mind you, I was not a religious person, but every song struck a nerve with my emotions. This station was my salvation, not only because of the music but also for the inspirational stories. It was the only music I listened to and still do today. I then went for a walk around the block to regain my composure. By the time I went back in. a few employees were there. Of course, I got the usual "condolences" and "welcome back." This made me very emotional so I went back outside. I came back a few minutes later and gathered my reports then headed out for the day. It was a tough day but I got through it. In my job, I encounter a lot of clients who are going through many difficult situations. The job can be emotionally draining as I hear many sad stories. I try to listen and help when I can. This also tapped into the little strength I had to get through my own problems. The first two days were very tough.

Now it was September 7th. I went to work but I admit I was totally focused on my psychic reading that evening so I could talk to Shirl. I finished taking care of my house chores by four o clock. I waited at my table until six so I could call for the reading. It seemed like days and all the while I was getting questions ready in my mind to ask her. I now started crying, worried she wouldn't come through. At six, I called and waited for her to come through. The first contact was my mom. She said she loved me, which blew me away. My mom wanted me to know that she is still very happy with her skin. Robin asked me if I understood. I explained that my mom had baby skin on her face even at 82 years old when she passed. This told me she was actually coming through. My father came through next. He wanted to tell me he loved me and was proud of me. He also told me to keep the tool boxes as they would be worth a lot of money. I knew it was him because he was an auto mechanic and I have his tools and equipment. Then my two sisters came through, telling me they loved me and thanked me for all my love and support. Mind you, I was very happy to hear from all of them, but I was waiting for Shirl. I was afraid I'd run out of time with the reading.

Then Robin said Shirl was waiting till everyone else came through. This was typical for her to stand back. She always stayed in the background due to her quiet nature. She started by saying how much she loves me. She also wanted to thank me for what I did to help her during her illness and passing. She also knows how much I love her and said no one had cared for her that much in her life. She reassured me that I did everything right. Shirl told me she loved the way I set up the room as she could see and hear all. Shirl then said something that verified to me that she was coming through. She said she enjoyed our dances. I started sobbing. Robin tried to console me. After I gathered my emotions Shirl told me to get rid of her clothes but keep her jewelry and family items because someone may want them. This referred to her two sons who were estranged for numerous reasons—lifestyles, drugs, thefts—all of which are no longer important. Shirl then said I was to keep her car as it was in better condition than mine. She told me again she loves me and she wants me to have a happy life. Shirl then said she tried to keep the pictures organized. I knew she was referring to my frantic search for the pictures shortly after her death. After that, I thanked you for the flowers that were blooming out of season. Shirl said, "Remember, you have to nurture the plants to get flowers." I knew exactly what she meant as she always took care of them because I either watered them too much or too little. I told Shirl I will always love her and I would talk to her again. When the reading was over, I was emotionally spent. Robin stayed on the phone telling me I had to let Shirl go and give up the dancing eventually as Shirl wants me to be happy by moving on with my life. I then asked if I could setup another reading in October. Robin said it's best to wait at least six months to allow for grieving. She told me to call in March. I thanked her and we hung up. I wanted to talk to Shirl in October as both our birthdays were in that month. I was very upset but I set my sights on March 2017.

Now I knew I had to get rid of my car. So when I went back to work, I asked my coworkers if they knew of anyone looking for a car. I ended up selling it for seven hundred dollars to a coworker. Now back to focusing on work. I started the same every day. I arrived early; got my schedule; and then went outside to walk, cry, and gather my emotions to perform my job. One Friday morning, even though it was pouring rain, I took my usual walk. While walking along the fence of the adjacent building, amongst all the trash and debris, I saw what looked like a book. The cover was gray and totally swollen from all the rain. I didn't touch it and continued on my walk. During that day and through that night, I couldn't get the book off my mind. I felt bad that it was abandoned so I decided that if the book was still there the next day, I would pick it up and see what it was. The next morning, I went looking for the book. Almost in relief, it was there. I picked it up, turned it over, and saw it was a Bible. The pages were all soaked. Not being versed in the Bible, I checked and noticed a ribbon marking a page. I carefully opened to where the ribbon marker was. I started looking at the page. It was 1 Corinthians chapter 13 and verses 4 through 8 were circled. I started reading the first pas- sage. It began, "Love is patient and kind" (1 Cor. 13:4). I totally lost it and started sobbing uncontrollably, I could barely see through the tears. I went to my car and continued to cry while I read the other numbered passages. I knew this was a sign from Shirl. *Wow!*

After reading them, I decided to dry out the book. I laid it open on the passenger seat. This book stayed in my car for at least a month before it dried out completely. All the pages were puffed up, but I didn't care. Eventually, I knew I had to keep it somewhere safe so I took the book in the house and laid it open on my kitchen counter. I propped it up and put two very important pictures of us next to it. Every day, I read it and continued looking for signs from Shirl, almost to an obsessive level. I would see coins, cardinals, and many feathers, which I hung from my rearview mirror where they are to this day. About a week later, I was sitting in my car on the side of the road and waiting to go into work. When the sun shone on the windshield, to my amazement, there were two footprints right in front of me on the glass. They even had the holes (nail markings). I was flabbergasted! I was completely overwhelmed and started sobbing. I figured it was a sign showing me she was walking with me. I looked at them all the time and decided not to wash the glass until they were gone. This was difficult as I am a smoker. The glass got smoky in a short period, but the footprints stayed there for three months.

Over the next few weeks, I started to get more depressed as important dates were coming up. My birthday was October 3rd, her birthday was October 16th. I tried not to think about mine, now it was hers. I thought about what I might do on that day. Kathy, my confidant and good friend, gave me the idea to buy Shirl a balloon. I accepted her suggestion, went to buy one, and made her a personal birthday card telling her how much I love and miss her. On the 16th, I took the balloon with the card attached and went outside. I wished her a happy birthday then released the balloon into the air. I watched it float away. It stayed in view for almost ten minutes. I spent the rest of the day crying. I continued to work, though I was still very depressed. I tried to keep my emotions private, though I knew everyone saw them. One day, near the end of November, I was coming down a porch stairway after finishing an inspection and as I hit the bottom step, I saw what I thought was a penny. When I picked it up, I noticed it was a charm from a necklace. It was the sign of the zodiac for October, Libra. Unbelievable, Shirl and mine's birthday sign! I then turned it over and the name "Alex" was engraved there. Remember, her African grey's name is Alex. This started another a crying fit so I rushed to my car where I sat for at least fifteen minutes while I tried to gather myself before going to the next inspection. Well, I made it through the day. When I got home, I threaded it on a purple ribbon and hung it on my rearview mirror where it still is to this day. These signs and symbols I was receiving kept reinforcing her presence with me.

Now it was getting close to Thanksgiving. I was so depressed, I wasn't going to prepare the holiday meal. I would just have a sandwich, which was my usual diet. I started to feel bad for the animals as we always shared the meal with them. So I decided to make a small meal. While I got the table ready, I had the idea to set a place for Shirl also. I even went so far as to fill her plate as well as mine and the birds. I know it sounds stupid, but I conversed with her during the meal, even asking her if everything was okay. This was my state of mind that every day I talked to her as if she was still home. December was tough as I was dealing with my bipolar issues as well as my loss. I spoke to France and told her I was so depressed and how much I needed to talk to Shirl. I shared with France and Franni that I was not happy with Robin who kept telling me I had to let go of Shirl. France then told me she had met a new psychic, Marie, at a conference they attended recently. I asked where she was from. She said she lives in Southwick. I went great as it was only forty minutes away from me so I could go for a face-to-face reading. I then asked if she thought it was okay for me to go to another person for a reading and she said it was. She gave me the phone number for Marie. I then placed a call to Marie, leaving a message that I would like to arrange a reading with her if possible. Marie was very nice. She was even willing to come to my house for the reading. I thanked her but said I would come to her as I have no space for visitors with the animals. We set up the reading for March 25th, our wedding anniversary, at six o'clock.

I was a little relieved after the call. I went to the doctor as I was still in a full-blown manic phase. This was only the second time since I was diagnosed twenty-eight years ago that I had a true manic phase. I was going to the psychiatrist every five days, but nothing seemed to help. I told myself I had to keep going till October 30, 2017, when I could bury her. Then I could end my life of unbearable pain. Well, Christmas came and went, though I truly don't remember how. Shortly after that, I received more devastating news. My sister Lisa, who lived in Florida with her husband David, had been diagnosed with brain cancer. I didn't know how much more I could I take. Lisa started chemo in January. I kept in touch with her regularly, trying to keep her spirits up. We didn't talk about the illness but I got updates through David. He had her at home and was caring for her with the assistance of a hospice.

Now it was March. My focus turned to the 25th, our wedding anniversary, and my next reading. I called Marie to verify our appointment. The week went horribly. On the 24th, I was in an accident, which caused over five thousand dollars in damage even though the vehicle was still drivable. Now I had to find a thousand dollars for the insurance deductible. I had to schedule the repairs that would take a week so I had to rent a car not covered by my insurance, which was an additional two hundred fifty dollars. *Wow!* On the day of my reading with Shirl, I arrived at her house at six and spent two hours with her. There were contacts with my mother, father, two sisters (Linda and Michele), and, of course, Shirl. This time, Shirl came through first. Shirl said she never felt so loved and can't express her love enough. She knew when she met me, I was the one for her forever. She thanked me again for all I did for her with her illness and told me to stop beating myself up as nothing would have changed the outcome. She wanted me to stop yelling at the animals as they are still grieving and confused. She said she wants love back in the home. Shirl thanked me for the birthday card and balloon I released on her birthday. The items are with her. Shirl then said she sees the table with items on it next to the bed that brings only tears but hopefully will change in time. I had her urn next to the bed with some pictures and a commemorative butterfly lamp which I talk to every night while crying. Shirl said she is there with me every night. She said try to be grateful for all the good times we shared. She was trying to help me but I needed to stay grounded by and come through as a family with the animals to show her we will make it. Then she said a house is just a house, but ours was a home due to the love we shared. If I needed to sell it though, her love follows me and will be with me wherever I go. Then she got quiet to let others come through. My mother came through saying she loved me and was always close and very proud of me. Mom said she loved sitting on the deck with her coffee.

While writing this portion of my story, the song "Years" by Barbara Mandrell started playing. I was reduced to tears and had to stop writing. Sorry for the interruption but, you see, all their love comes through signs all the time. Where was I?

Oh yeah, my mother told me she was okay with whatever I did regarding Grete, my youngest sister. My mom asked me a few years before she died to give Grete three items for her grandchildren (Grete's children) after her death: my mother's ring for Erika, the cross for Marion, and Dad's wedding band for Morgan. I still planned on getting them to Grete as I promised my mom I would. I just didn't know when or how as we were estranged (long story) and still weren't talking. I need to explain a little further. You see, Shirl's son Duane was married to my sister Grete for five years. Shirl and my mother were the grandparents of Grete and Duane's children. The details are too complicated to go into and not important now. Once it ended in divorce, there was bitterness, anger, and devastation, which left the families in turmoil. So there were a lot of issues that kept me from contacting Grete. The resolution came later.

My dad came through next and sent his love saying, "Love you, baby" as he always called me baby. Linda came through with love, thanking me for how I tried to help her daughter Tammy emotionally (again, a complicated story). Linda said it was time to move on. Michele, though very quiet, sent her love. After they came through, Shirl came back. She said again that flowers only bloom when the plants are nurtured. The flowers were still blooming at home. Then she said, "Follow your intuition, trust your gut, and don't second guess yourself when making important decisions." Shirl then said she wanted me to have something special on the anniversary of her death as I needed to have something for me. She told me to get a piece of cheesecake, which she knew was my favorite dessert, and that there would be two new people coming into my life. I said okay and asked her if I was hurting her by holding her back and dancing with her. She said I could dance with her every day if I wanted. I told her I will love her forever and would talk to her again. Shirl closed by telling me the door is always open for me to talk to her and she loves me. Then the reading ended.

 I thanked Marie, telling her I would call to schedule a reading in August. I spent some time absorbing everything that was said. I felt a little better with her love and reassurance that she is always with me but I was still depressed as she wasn't here physically. Marie called me that night to setup a date and time. I asked for August 7, the day Shirl passed away, but she only had August 10 available. I agreed. I felt relieved after the call and went back to the present and back to work.

 Early April, I got a letter from Cary from the hospice, telling me the senior center was trying to set up a grief group at the end of April and asked if I was interested in going. I called her and said yes. I got a call around the fifteenth from Cary saying that the group did not have enough people, so they would have to try again in the fall. I thanked her for thinking about me. I got very depressed as I was looking forward to being with people who understood my grief. Well, I told Cary to call me if it happened in the fall. I kept working and doing everything I needed to do to move forward in life. I got a call at the end of April. They now had enough people for the group to start. She said the first meeting was on Wednesday, the 3rd of May. It would run for seven weeks. I said I would go. After I hung up, I was excited and thought how it was meant to be.

 I called David in the first week of May. He said Lisa was really deteriorating and wasn't coherent. I asked David to put the phone to her ear so I could speak to her. I told her how my I loved her and I was sorry that our relationship had become estranged due to complicated family issues, but I stressed to her that I will always love her. I then thanked David for letting me talk to her. I told him I would call every night to see how both of them were doing. I knew firsthand how devastating it is for the caregiver to watch the life (spirit) of a loved one fading away in front of you and there is nothing you can do to stop it. On May 11th, I was sitting in my car waiting to go into work when David called to inform me that Lisa passed away. I started crying and told him how sorry I was. David told me he would let me know about the funeral arrangements. Crying in my car, I asked God how much more would I have to take. My mother died January 10, 2014; my sister Michele died March 10, 2014; Michele's daughter, my niece, died March 22, 2015; then Shirl died August 7, 2016; and now Lisa died on May 11, 2017.

I didn't think I could handle any more loss. I had five days for bereavement. I contacted my Dr. as I was slipping further into depression. I saw him once a week over the next two months. He was trying to stabilize my condition. I was in and out of manic phase and nothing seemed to help my state of mind. I kept in touch with David though as I knew he had no family to help him either. He did have Debbie, Lisa's closest friend, and her husband John. They came down from New York shortly before she died and stayed a while after to help him with the arrangements and console him. I kept telling him there are no words to help him, only that she loved him. I told him to open his mind and pay attention to his surroundings as I'm sure she was sending signs of love. I called him every night to talk about our losses. During one conversation, I told him I was enrolled in a grief group starting at the end of May and suggested that he look into it through hospice. He said he'd think about it. The conversations were very intense that reduced me to tears. David would get quiet so I know I hit deep nerves. At one point, I told him if I was hurting him too much that I would stop calling. David said I should keep calling, and I did. We learned that our lives with our spouses were very much parallel. We kept to ourselves, doing everything and enjoying our times together. We were both very depressed. Many nights, we didn't see life getting any better. The grief was intense.

From the many conversations, it was comfort to know we were not alone because we shared the devastation over our losses. At least had work; he was retired.

At the first group session on May 31, I arrived early. As I always did, I was sitting in my car, nervous if I could speak to strangers about my private emotions. Then a voice came to my head saying I should just do it. The session went okay. I felt accepted. France and Franni were also in the group, which comforted me a little. During the second group session, I told everyone I had psychic readings with Shirl, which comforted me as I was going through my grief. We all shared our emotions over our losses. Even though we had different situations, it helped that there was a connection between us all. Time flew as I continued to juggle my finances, work, and attending the grief group. By June, my car was repaired. I still talked to David every night and looked for signs from Shirl. July came fast. The last session was upon me. I was a little sad it was ending as the group kept me from isolating myself, which helped me with my depression.

After the last group meeting, I turned my focus to August 10, 2017, my next reading with Shirl. I took the whole week off from work to grieve the one year anniversary of her death. Three days before the next reading, I bought myself a piece of cheesecake, just as she told me last March. That was extremely tough as she was the one that always bought it for me on special occasions. I got through the day by myself, crying the whole time. On August 10, I met with Marie. When the reading started, Marie said Shirl's energy was extremely strong, which was sending chills through her entire body. She extended her tremendous love for me and reiterated that she was always with me. She said she sends messages through Alex so I should listen for new words. Marie then said, "She's calling you 'babe'." This hit home. I started sobbing as this was verification that she was really there because I never told anyone that she called me that when she expressed her affection for me. She added that I should pay attention at night when she brushes my hair and comes to me with her whole being (soul). Also, I should not dismiss the thoughts entering my mind. She then said I need to do something with my life though as she knew why I was reclusive and that the seventh was always difficult for me.

She said I had to take care of myself. She went on to say she did all she could for me and she was very happy at peace, and without pain. Shirl said I needed to take supplement *ginkgo biloba* for memory. This will help to clarify my path. I also was to increase the protein (eggs for breakfast) in my diet.

Wow, this blew my mind! Marie was also stunned. Shirl went on to say she missed our talks. Then she said the pond was special, which was next to her plot where I promised to bury her remains on October 30. She said she was blessed to have me and she has my back. Shirl then addressed Duane, her son, saying that I don't need to try and fix his problems. But if I see him, she sends her love. She acknowledged the special flowers I planted in the garden this summer around the wishing well we bought the summer before she died. She said the house would get better as money was coming in. She acknowledged our wedding rings. I wore hers on my left pinky next to mine. I click them together when I need her to let her know I'm thinking of her. Shirl said my finances will get better soon and advised not to be afraid to ask anyone for help. Shirl repeated that there were two new people coming into my life. She hoped I would find someone else to love. She assured me that even though it would not be as deep as our love, it's okay as she was waiting for me. Shirl said something about a school teacher in my life. This had no meaning to me. Again she told me I could dance with her every day if I wanted. Finally, she said I would be whole and happy again. Shirl backed off for another to come through.

Lisa, who passed away last May, was next. She said she loved me and she was very sorry that our relationship was estranged. She did not accept Shirl and my relationship while she was alive, but she now knows what a loving relationship we had. She also said she had no right to judge and expect me to give up on the person that I loved. She said sorry again. I thanked her then asked if she had any messages for David. She said she loves him and thanks him for his care as she never felt more loved. She was standing behind him in the bathroom mirror, but he was not paying attention. Lisa went on to say if David needed to leave the house, it was okay. September will be special. David was going on a trip with Debbie and John, their friends for years, to a place where Lisa and he had gone.

Next was my mom, sending her love and telling me she was proud of me. She then told me she would not have been able to forgive people who hurt her as I did. Mom told me she was all right with whatever decision I make with the jewelry. Mom then said, "Don't worry about money, a promotion was coming." She finished by saying she will be waiting for me with Shirl. Dad sent his love. He said he didn't mean to aggravate me so much but he liked to play. He said he was proud of me touching many students' lives more than I knew. I taught at a trade school for a year but decided it was not a good fit for me. Linda, Michele, and her daughter came through, sending their love. They were part of my fan club.

Shirl came back saying that I had to go to Gardner State Park where we had our first date. She said that on September 16, I was to bring something and leave it, but also take something. This date represented when we got married the first time (we got married twice, 1996 and 2014) at the first congregational church in Amherst, Massachusetts. She then said the Libra-Alex charm I found was a gift. Again, she admonished that I have to eat better. Shirl echoed what my mom said about a special recognition and at least two promotion opportunities that were coming my way as I was highly respected by many. These things had no meaning to me at that time other than I had started looking for a new job. Then she said that in December, I would be much more in tune (closer) to her. She again closed with she loved me and was always with me.

As the reading ended, I thanked Marie and set up a new reading for October 30, the day of Shirl's funeral. With that done, I went home and started going over what Shirl had said in the reading. First thing was to figure out what to bring to the park on September 16. I decided to take a picture and made a sign that said "Forever soul mates." When September came, I was listening to the news when they said that due to budget issues, Gardner State Park would be closed. *Oh no! Now what?* I decided I would take a chance and go anyway.

On September 16, I headed for the park, a forty-minute drive, with my gifts. As I approached the area, I saw barrier gates blocking the parking lot. I turned my car around and parked on the shoulder of the road. Now I debated if I could sneak in to do what I had to do. There were a few houses nearby that could see me if I entered the area. I didn't know if someone would call the police for trespassing. Well, it was now or never. I grabbed my items and a screwdriver and went in. I picked a tree that I could hide behind and mounted the two items. After I finished, I looked around to see if there was anything on the ground—maybe a coin, feather, or something. I noticed a very large red maple leaf. This drew me as red was Shirl's favorite color. I picked up the leaf and went back to my car. I cried for about five minutes then thanked Shirl and left.

When I got home, I didn't know what to do with the leaf. It came to me to put the date on it, slathered it with shellac, and put it on display next to the Bible on my counter in the kitchen. I felt better after I went to the park. It made me feel closer to her. Now my mind was set on October. Our birthdays were coming again as well as her burial. I had reached the point in my life where I had to think of myself. This was very difficult as I was always the caregiver for everyone in my family. If there was a problem, I would take the bull by the horns and try to fix it. Now I had to take care of myself. I just kept saying aloud, "But I don't know how!"

Thinking of the Future

During this time, I started thinking about my purpose in life. I thought about volunteering with the Easthampton senior center. I remembered saying for years that when I retired, I would volunteer to deliver meals. I also thought about the Meals on Wheels program as they only delivered during the weekdays. I wondered what the seniors did on the weekends.

Over the next two weeks, I went to the center to see if there were any programs on the weekends. I was told they weren't aware of any. About this time a manager came over. I explained what I wanted to do for seniors. He then said they just got funding for a shopping program for home bound seniors. There was a grocery store that allowed shopping on delayed payments. The groceries would be purchased and delivered then the family would make out a check to be submitted to the store. I asked how to become a volunteer. He said they would have to submit to a CORI check. If accepted, the volunteer would contact the family in need and make arrangements for the day of the week, time, and grocery list. I was told the volunteer would be paid mileage. I told him to donate it to the center as I didn't want anything. He said they couldn't take it. I asked, "if you pay me, can I just give you the check?" He said he didn't know if it would be a conflict. I decided not to accept the money. My purpose was to volunteer. I filled out the application and asked how long it would take to see if I qualified. He said about two weeks. I thanked him and left. I felt good after leaving and waited for the decision. While I waited for a response, I went back to my other duties at work and at home.

The beginning of October was here. On my birthday, I went to work then and bought a few scratch tickets. When I went home, I saw the birthday card that Shirl bought me before she died, which I keep on my counter. As I read the card, I was reminded of her great love for me. Though she was not here, it brought me some comfort. The second week, I heard from the center that I was accepted. I was told they were in the process of qualifying seniors in need as they also had to qualify. Linda was the representative and she told me to wait for her call once there was a qualifying family. So I had to wait again.

Now Shirl's birthday was upon me. I went to Walmart. At the card section, I spent fifteen minutes going through all the cards but I couldn't find the right one so I started crying. Just then, a card stuck out to me. This was it! Then I went to the bakery and bought a small cake. At the checkout counter, the cashier tried ring out the card but the SKU (stock keeping unit) number wouldn't read. She tried at least five times. At that moment, I said to Shirl I was getting this card. Then the supervisor was called, again the SKU wouldn't go through. Finally, after almost five minutes, the supervisor punched in a general SKU and I got the card. I thanked them and left the store. I then went to a variety store and purchased some scratch tickets. This was what we bought each other every year. I put the scratch tickets in with her card and went home. I made supper for the parrots and a sandwich for myself. After that, I took the card, put a candle on the cake, placed them on the table, and greeted her a happy birthday. I cut two pieces of cake and sat down. With the tickets next to her cake, I wished her luck. I scratched the tickets, crying all the while. She ended up with over thirty dollars. The amount was not important, I just wanted to feel close to her.

With her burial coming soon, I was so depressed. Around the eighteenth, I went to the florist and ordered two dozen each of her favorite flowers, red-and-yellow gladiolus and carnations. I was to pick them up on the thirtieth at eight in the morning. Next, I called the funeral home as I had not heard from the pastor about the service. I finally met with her on the twenty-fifth. I told her about Shirl's personality, life, and what passages of scripture I wanted read. It was all set. I also gave the funeral director Shirls' ashes for the day of burial. Now on the twenty-eighth, I called Marie, the psychic, to confirm my reading on the thirtieth at six o'clock. That day, the weather channel was forecasting a storm starting on the twenty-ninth. Snow and strong winds would last into the thirtieth. *Oh no!* There was no way I could cancel Shirl's funeral that day. I called her brother and sister and told them if they couldn't come, I'd understand as they were some distance away. Her brother said he wouldn't make it due to his health. Her sister said she'd try.

    The morning of the thirtieth, it was snowing, and the winds were in excess of 25 mph with gusts over 40 mph. I was concerned no one would come but deep inside, I knew it was okay. I was told for years that when a person is buried during bad weather, they are at peace. I was the first to arrive at the cemetery around eight in the morning with flowers in tow. Mind you, the service was set for nine o'clock but I'm always early. I sat in my car nervously waiting, not knowing if anyone else would come. To my relief, people I invited started showing up. It was now 8:45 a.m. The funeral director arrived with Shirl. We waited for the pastor who arrived a few minutes later. A total of thirteen people were at the service. This number will be significant in my next psychic reading with Shirl that evening. At this point, I told the pastor I had a song I wanted to play near the end of the service, our wedding song, "I Swear." During the service, the sleet came down with a vengeance and the wind was whipping at least 40 mph. I was soaked. Just before Shirl's body was laid in the earth, I turned the song on. I fell to my knees, sobbing and shaking, while I sang the song to her. Friends helped me up and everyone consoled me as the service ended. I thanked all who came. After everyone left, I personally thanked the funeral director and pastor for all their help. When they left, I stayed behind. Finally alone, I knelt at her grave, sobbing, and asked if the service was okay. A short time later, I headed home. Now my work was done. She was buried, and it was final.

    Around five, I left home for my psychic reading. Marie welcomed me an hour later. Shirl was the first one through. She acknowledged that it was a beautiful service and the pastor was very loving. She noticed her family wasn't there. Marie then said the number fourteen is coming from Shirl regarding the service. I told her there were thirteen people there. Shirl insisted on fourteen again. I then counted again and got thirteen. She then said I didn't count her.

Marie said she was seeing a red rose. This meant Shirl sends her love. Shirl said she loved me with all her heart and we had such good times together. Shirl saw the picture I left at the park. She also said our time driving along the coast of Maine was a special memory. Shirl said I was going down a new road of healing and the rain (tears) helps with the healing. I would experience new strength. Shirl then said she was showing herself through the light flickering on the living room ceiling. I took videos of the strange light wondering if it was her. She was also happy with what I put in the urn with her. I had the funeral home put all the ashes from our animals in with her ashes, all seven of them. Then she said there was writing for me on a mirror. I didn't understand, but she said I will figure it out. Shirl congratulated me for my new boss. I couldn't believe she knew that. She said he will be good as he has respect for me. Shirl insisted a new job or promotion is in my future.

Lisa then came through, telling me to keep nudging him to move on and try to be happy. She acknowledged the trike idea. David took his Harley and modified it into a tricycle. Lisa told me to send her love to him. My mom then came through, telling me she loves me and is very proud of me. Shirl came back through, saying she sees the road I am going down. "There will be help for the volunteer work, just keep pushing and asking for help." Shirl said I will heal and my confidence will grow, as well as my power. I will also get peace. Then she said I made her life brighter by accepting her and allowing her to be herself, good and bad. She said I was doing great and she's got my back. She also was happy I enjoyed the cheesecake. Shirl told me to be open to abundance and there is a higher good. I told her I love and miss her, but we'll talk again in March. Then the reading ended. I thanked Marie and left for home.

The next day, I took the whole week off. I went over the reading and wondered what she meant by "abundance" and a "higher good." I was thumbing through the TV channels and stopped at a network I did not know, Trinity Broadcasting Network (TBN). There was a guy speaking about how God loves us. He said, "You need to say to yourself that you are a child of God and you are valued." Well, this reduced me to tears so I kept watching and listening to the pastor's words. They cut straight to my heart. That entire morning, I watched the channel as different pastors spoke. It was like every word was meant for me. After that, I started thinking about returning to church. But which one? I was raised Catholic, though I turned away many years ago because of the abuse scandals. Then it came to me. Shirl and I got married in the Easthampton Congregational Church in 2014. That's it! I will try going there. I decided to go on the first Sunday of November. In the meantime, I focused on the volunteer work and my job. I received a call for a client to shop for. I got the information and called the client, Daniel, on Friday. I delivered the groceries to him and his mother who was ninety-one years old. I felt really good helping them. I told Daniel I would call for the list every Friday and shop on Saturday. Great! I waited for more clients in need.

On Sunday, I headed off to church for the ten o'clock service. As I waited, I read the weekly bulletin on the service. I saw that every first Sunday was communion day. I felt nervous as I didn't feel worthy to receive communion. During the service, I looked at my watch. It was already after eleven. I didn't know how much longer it would last. I had to be home by noon to dance with Shirl. The service which ended at 11:25 a.m. I made it home in time as I only lived only ten minutes away. At home, I waited for noon. As I danced with Shirl, I told her I went to church and would continue to go. As the next few weeks went by, I continued to watch TBN whenever I could. It became an obsession. I kept going to church and shopping for Daniel. Now Thanksgiving was here again. I couldn't believe how fast time flies. I was still alive and moving forward, still depressed but no longer suicidal. The day went okay. I made a small dinner and again set a plate for Shirl.

On the first weekend of December, I received the final bill from the funeral home. It was less than it should have been so I wrote a check and added an extra hundred dollars for their services to thank them for everything.

Spiritual Awakening

On December 3, I was sitting at my table, looking at Shirl's picture, and sobbing that another Christmas was coming and she wasn't here with me. I was trying to decide whether to decorate for Christmas. Right then, a strong voice suddenly came over me. *You should be celebrating her life, not mourning her death. Wow!* I hear you. I sat there with my head down. At that moment, there was major shift in my life. I got up, went to the basement, and brought up the decorations. I pulled out the thirty-five stockings, one for each pet we had, hers and mine. I hung them all up along the plant shelf in the living room. Mind you, the shelf was twelve feet long. Good thing as there wasn't room after I was done. I was overwhelmed by what we had. I then set up the ceramic Christmas tree my father made thirty years ago.

After I was done, I looked it over and realized I had so many blessings while we together. It was at this moment that I gave my life to the Lord. I prayed for forgiveness and asked Jesus to come into my life. Of course I was crying as usual, but for the first time since Shirl died, I felt calm. I now knew it was a new beginning in my life. I decided at that point that I needed to be thankful for everything I had with her and for my life. I also wanted to buy a Bible and start reading God's word. About a week later, I received a card from the funeral home. Inside was a note saying they donated fifty dollars to the Dakin animal shelter in Shirl's name and a gift card for fifty dollars. *Wow*, I couldn't believe this was happening to me! I dropped my head and thanked God for the blessing. With the gift card, I bought my Bible and a daily devotional book. Every morning when I got up, I read the message in my devotional. I also started praying every night in bed. I always believed in God, but now I had a personal relationship with the Lord. I decided to surrender my life to Jesus. I sobbed when I asked him to forgive me. I wanted to receive his grace. At that moment, I felt a sense of peace. I told Jesus I truly love him. I didn't know what his purpose for me was, but where he leads, I will follow. It was so easy to talk to him, as if I was talking to my best friend. I said, "No one knows me like you, Lord, and even with all my faults, I am so loved."

Now let me tell you what Jesus has done for me in my life since my shift. Mid-December, I was getting ready to order my prescriptions for my bipolar. A strong voice said, "You don't need them anymore." *What?* "Again, you don't need them. You are well." At that moment, I accepted in faith what I was told and I didn't refill them. Every day, I kept reading the Bible and thanking Jesus for my healing. I asked for help in healing my broken heart. I went about my days, working and volunteering. I told David my encounter with the Lord. He said it was good, but I could tell when people doubt. That's okay. I kept moving forward.

On December 23, I received bad news. I got a summons to appear in court on March 29, 2018, as Discover was suing me for the card debt. The thing is, I really wasn't that upset. On Christmas Eve, I decorated the tree and then danced with Shirl. It was very intimate and calming. I prayed to Jesus every day for guidance and answers. I put this problem in his hands as this was bigger than me. I knew he could take care of it. All I did was get my documents together and waited for court date. I still couldn't believe I wasn't even anxious, though a few times I thought about trying to resolve it before court. I then realized Jesus was truly moving in my life. I started thanking God for the many blessings he had given me. Christmas was still hard, but I survived. I made a dinner for me and the birds and set a plate for Shirl. After supper, I thought about the birth of Jesus. I then decided to give him a birthday card. I picked out a card that had a picture of him being held in his mother's arms. I wrote in the card, "Welcome, Jesus. All my love." I hung the card with the Lord's picture on my wall across from my bed, where it remains to this day. After Christmas, I got ready for my next psychic reading on the 29th.

At my next reading, Shirl came plowing through. She said the end of the year would be better with Grete. She said she continues to visit Alex and she was happy he is much calmer now. Shirl said she felt very close to me during our dance on Christmas Eve. Shirl then blew me away, telling me the Lord hears my prayers. She then said there was something coming on the house. I didn't know what she meant till the March reading. Shirl then acknowledged a new baby somewhere. I had my new great-grandniece. She sent her love. Shirl said about half of the debt would be settled before court. She said 2018 would be much better and I was mentally stronger now since her death. Regarding my volunteer work, she said there would be four more people to help by the end of 2018 and that I would get a new car within the next two years. Shirl mentioned some kind of promotion, possibly new department in same company. Then she said I was getting better, a perfect mind. I had no clue what she was talking about. Then I realized this was a reference to my bipolar condition. I no longer have the condition. This was my first spiritual healing from Jesus. Praise the Lord as there have been many since. Then she said there was writing for me in the mirror. Marie asked if I had noticed anything. I said no. Shirl said to watch for it as it is there. Shirl said there are many spirits behind me, moving me forward. I was to stay patient and wait for the answers. Shirl then told me about the deaths of some of our animals. I was told Sparky, Lil Bit, and Ember will go this year. I was to bury them in the pet cemetery in the yard. She then said the den will be beautiful with it's done. She then interpreted a dream I had. The black cat represented peace and the white patch on the cat represented the heart. She said to pay attention to the number of birds (crows). There was not as many cardinals anymore as she is always with me. She said to look up the spiritual reference to the frog. Then she said the number eight has significance. Shirl then backed away as my mother and father came through. Lisa came next, saying David was not feeling her or hearing her because he was in a dark place. But she was there with him, waiting for him when he's ready. Michele sent her love. She's is in a good place. Then Shirl came back to say, "Don't listen to doubters. Be true to yourself."

When the session ended. I set up a new reading on March 22, 2018, and left for home. I checked the spiritual meanings for the number eight and the hawk. I was amazed. Both mean "new beginnings" and "regeneration." This was exactly how I was feeling. I then checked on the frog. Some church readings referenced relying totally on God and the community. There was even a reference to a finished room.

Spiritual Growth

At the beginning of January, I decided to read my Bible. Mind you, I have never read it. I decided to start at the very beginning. Every night, I read for an hour from five to six. I started to learn and understand God's Word. I also had prayer time every night at bedtime. I started to evaluate my life. I realized I needed to let go of the past. I forgave the people in my life who had deeply hurt me. I then asked God to forgive me for the people I hurt along the way. I truly started to feel an inner sense of peace. The more I read God's word, the calmer I felt. I asked Jesus to help me understand what my purpose was in this life. After my prayers, I again spoke to Shirl. I thanked God for letting her go first so she did not suffer the pain that I have gone through. I realized she would have had a very difficult time living alone—not financially, but with no outside support. I thanked God for allowing Shirl in my life for thirty-one years. I now knew God works in very mysterious ways and does all things for good.

Every morning and night, I asked Jesus to fill me with the Holy Spirit for wisdom, guidance, and understanding to fulfill God's purpose for my life. I continued asking Jesus to help me with my financial situation regarding the Discover card debt. I knew he would take care of it. I then thanked him and continued to watch different pastors on TBN. I couldn't seem to get enough of God's word. I bought an audio Bible, which I keep in my car. I listen from 6:30 to 7:15 a.m. before I get to work. I continued to attend church and noticed I was calmer and at peace within. I had no worries and I moved at a slow and steady pace. As I learned more and more, I started noticing many little things. While driving, I realized I was hitting mostly green lights. It may sound funny, but you know when you're in a hurry and you hit all red. I learned not to get ahead of the

Lord. I was going to work one morning, I was not paying attention so I was pulled over for speeding. The officer asked me if I knew how fast I was going. I said no. He said 48 mph in a 30-mph zone. As I waited for the ticket, I thanked Jesus for slowing me down. I then thanked the officer. I put the ticket on my dash where it sits to this day. All the way to work, I thanked the Lord for the warning. I started to see hawks at work and I thanked Jesus for all my blessings.

On March 22, 2018, I went for another reading with Shirl. She came through with her love and acknowledged our anniversary. She said that the room in the back will be a closed by the fall. I knew that she was talking about the renovation I was trying to do. I wanted to add a den or sanctuary, a place where I can have a quiet Bible time and watch the birds and stars all year around. She then talked about our dancing rituals. She said it would be different now. I knew what she meant. Two weeks ago, a voice told me that the dances will celebrate special times now, not focus on the Sundays marking her death. *Wow!* I was taken back but understood the message. She said I was now hearing a higher voice. I asked her if I would be going on a trip. I had a voice come through prior to my reading, telling me to go to Israel. She said I would be going with two or three other church people possibly in the fall. This was amazing as I was interested in a trip planned by a ministry, which was sometime in November, but it was very expensive. I knew I still had to get my finances and credit straightened out. My plan was maybe in two years. I thanked Shirl for her support and love. Marie told me that I was so in tuned to her that I no longer needed to go for readings. Marie said it was like Shirl and I were together and she was just a bystander. I told Marie I would set our readings to two times a year instead of four. I still wanted the readings. We agreed on October 30 instead of August. I thanked Marie and left.

The next day, I decided to go fishing. I went to the store for bait then pond by the cemetery. As I knelt down and prayed, I saw the remnant of flowers from her burial. The withered plant was still lying on her gravestone. After talking to her and God, I picked up the bouquet and went to the pond. I used her pole and mine. It seemed like she was there even though I knew she was in spirit. Once

I was all set, I placed the flowers on top of the water then watched as they floated away. I decided to stay till they were out of my sight. Though I caught nothing it felt good to be near the water. Fishing was some of our best memories together. After an hour, the wind started blowing across the pond. I kept watching the flowers. Two hours later, I could no longer see them. I packed up, said I love you, and left.

The next week, I had that court date on Thursday, the twenty-ninth. The day before, I was driving to my inspections when a voice told me to call Discover one last time to try and settle before the court date. I kept thinking about the call as I had put this issue in the Lord's hands, but I didn't want Jesus to think my faith was waning. I pulled my car over and made the call. I was on with the representative for about fifteen minutes. By the end, we settled the debt for half of what was owed. I agreed to give a thousand dollars that day then make small monthly payments for five years, unless I could pay it sooner. I transferred the money from my savings to checking and made the payment. I started sobbing and thanking Jesus for blessing me again. With my financial debt problem settled, I thanked Jesus for giving me the answers. The amazing part of this story is that the following week when I checked my savings account balance, there was a thousand more than I should have had. It was as if the money I used for Discover wasn't taken out. I went back through all my statements and accounts. All deposits and withdrawals were accounted for. I knew Jesus blessed me again. I thanked the Lord. *Praise be to God!*

I now focused on my prayer life, continuously thanking Jesus for all my blessings, the new room, and the trip to Israel. Mind you, they haven't been done yet, but I have faith in Jesus as I know it will be done, though I don't know when. By April, my spiritual life was growing with God's word. I was reading and understanding more. I praised and thanked Jesus for everything every chance I got. I took the time to enjoy all things Jesus blessed me with. I acknowledged his presence at every opportunity throughout my day. I then started contemplating how much the additional room would cost and how long I needed to wait to go for financing. By mid-April, an inner voice told me to check on the cost. I called two contractors for bids.

The price would be between twenty-five and thirty-five thousand dollars. Having the price, I knew it would be difficult with my credit. I decided to apply anyway and went to my bank. I was told my credit score was 647, which she said was in the fair range so I filled out the application. The loan officer said I would know in about a week. As I left, I knew it was in Jesus' hands now as this was bigger than me. I waited patiently for the answer. Two weeks went by, no answer. I called the bank and was told it was still under review. Another week went by, then I got a call on May 8th. She said it was denied due to the very recent settlement with Discover card. I admit I was disappointed. She told me to try again in August in three months' time. It would help my credit rating. I thanked her and hung up. I thanked God even though it was not the answer I wanted to hear. The dream room was delayed status but I would continue in faith that if it was for my good and his glory, it will happen. I now told God I would continue to pursue this request and would reapply in July. I continued volunteering, shopping for my two clients, and going to church every week.

The first anniversary of my sister Lisa's death was coming up on May 11. I knew it was going to be a terrible week for my brother in-law. I have spoken to him nightly since she died. We talk for usually an hour. I told David the first death anniversary would be very tough and how I coped with the first anniversary of Shirl's death. It was almost worse than when she passed. I was so numb, it was surreal. Eventually, I accepted that she wasn't coming home.

Choosing Joy

My life started to become very focused and calm. I prayed every night for the room. I told the Lord it was his room and it was beautiful. I even picked out a name, Lily of the Valley. I then asked David to make me an engraved lily on a piece of wood so I could put a picture with some scripture on it and hang it above the doorway.

On the first Tuesday of May, I called Heddy, one of my clients, for her shopping list. She informed me that her sister who lives with her passed away over the weekend. I gave my condolences. I told her I would keep in touch and call the following week and offered for her to call me if she needed anything or just wanted to talk. That night, I prayed to the Lord to comfort Heddy and her family in this difficult time. Every night after my prayers, I turned on the butterfly light and spoke to Shirl as well as my family. But one night in mid-May, I told her I would see her again though I don't know when as things work in God's time, not mine. I asked her to save me a seat as I was going to be a little late. At the end of our talk, I would always say, "Good night, wherever you are." This time, I said, "I know where you are. You're in the most beautiful place with God."

I also had to schedule maintenance work on my car. I needed new brakes and a wheel bearing, a total cost $950. I thanked Jesus for blessing my finances to make the repairs. I scheduled work for last week of May for my vacation. I went fishing for two days and got the car fixed. The rest of the time, I just relaxed and continued to grow in my prayer life.

By the end of May, I was told by my pastor that they would be taking in new members in June and she would let me know the date. I was very happy. On the first Sunday of June, the pastor told me church that on June 10th, there would be a meeting to go over membership and I would be accepted as a new member on the 17th. I told her I was all in and would do as much as I could to help the church. I met with board members on the tenth to go over the history of the church and the mission of helping the community. I explained my family history, personal feelings, and passion for helping people. After our in-depth discussion, I was told the process of the ceremony to take place on June 17th. Over the next week, I thought of how great it will be to belong to community where I could help more people and engage with a church family in completing the mission for the Lord. Well, I was made a member of the church and given a Bible during the ceremony, which I did not expect. When I received it, I was overwhelmed and started crying. I was so happy. After the service, we all met in the fellowship hall for refreshments. I met other members and felt I was part of a family. I now felt great!

In the next two weeks I started planning a trip to see David in New York. I only had one day available on July 5th. I coordinated with the people who were going to take care of my animals. On July 2, my car exhaust went. I had to get it fixed then I realized there was no way I would be able to go on the trip. That night, I called David with the bad news. He was good about it. I told him maybe I could go during my vacation in August. I got the car fixed on the 5th, which cost six hundred dollars. I thanked God for the money to pay for it. Now I was still on the mission of building the additional room in my house. I prayed on it every night. I thanked Jesus and told him I named the room Lily of the valley. I looked up the spiritual meaning of the lily. Lo and behold! It meant humility and devotion. That was it! I wrote "Thank you, Lord, from your humble and devoted servant." I have faith that the Lord will move the mountain. I also know if it is meant to be, it will happen in God's time.

I put my sights on the home equity loan again. I reapplied in three months as the loan officer advised. I called and made the appointment in July. On July 20, I applied for the loan. My credit score jumped twelve points since April. I filled out the application and then waited for God's answer. I knew, one way or another, I would get the answer as he is always faithful. I continued to grow in my faith and spend time reading the Bible each day. I worked every day and continued shopping for my homebound clients. I was also looking for more ways to help the less fortunate people in the com- munity through my church. Now on July 25th, I received a call from the bank. Unfortunately, my credit score was two points below their requirement for approval. I thanked the loan officer for her time and said that I would apply again at a later date. After the call, I thanked the Lord for answering my prayer even though it was no. I was surprised that I was only slightly disappointed and accepted that it was not God's will for me at this time. I will not give up on the room, but I have put my faith in the Lord so I would continue to pray on it. If it was for my good and his glory, it will be done in God's own time. I continued to work and volunteer at the senior center. I also put my sights on finishing this book and find different ways to help people in the community through my church.

On August 2nd I was chosen by my employer to train with another department to help fill a temporary need. It would require more responsibilities in the office, doing rental negotiations between tenants and landlords. I also had to continue performing my current task as a housing inspector. I accepted the challenge and would start training the next day. On my drive home, I kept praising and thanking the Lord for another blessing. When I got home, I fell on my knees, thanking Jesus for leading me in this new endeavor. I then remembered my psychic reading with Shirl when she said there would be one or two promotion opportunities coming my way. *Wow, unbelievable!* I was on my knees, sobbing and thanking her for looking out for me and rooting for me.

I am now near the final chapter of my two-year journey. I know some of you may find it hard to believe the many twists and turns my life has taken. The many blessings I have written did happen, and this is my honest testimony. I did not add or embellish any parts of my story. I also want you to know that even though I wrote this book every day, I tell my story to anyone who will listen to my testimony of healing.

Season of Contentment

On August 7, 2018, two years to the day when my life was changed forever with the loss of Shirl, I look back and come to realize many things. First of all, I didn't expect to even be here as I planned for years that I would go before Shirl, to the point where I made sure she would be set financially when I passed away. We only talked about a few times as she would get upset and say the money means nothing because she would be all alone. I never really understood her statement until I had to suffer the pain of my loss. I have also come to realize that even though I thought I had it all figured out, the Lord had different plans that were above my comprehension, though I know one day it will all be revealed to me. I now thank God that Shirl went before me so she didn't have to suffer through the devastation that almost killed me. I *danced* with Shirl on this day because it is a very special occasion. It was filled with joyous tears instead of sorrow for I now know she is with the Lord.

After feeding the animals, I had an urge to go to the cemetery. I decided to cut one of her flowers, the peace lily. I also grabbed a 2018 penny then drove to the cemetery. As I put the lily in the ground and laid the penny on the marker, I said, "We are both at peace now." I thanked God again for having her in my life. I guess the Lord still had plans for me as I made it through the absolute lowest point in my life and was healed through my Lord Jesus Christ. Praise be to God! I now treasure every day the Lord allows me to be on this earth. I have learned there is healing after loss. Life is short, precious, and worth living. I pay more attention to all of God's wonderful creations every day. I especially take the time to reflect on the little things, such as the birds, flowers, sunrises, and sunsets. There are many things I have to be grateful for in my life as everything I have is from the grace of God. Most importantly, I am healthy in my mind, body, and soul. My animals are still healthy. I have a good job and a nice home. There are many other things I could write but they're too numerous to list. I now have inner peace and joy in my life. I only listen to the K-LOVE radio station now, which gives me so much inspiration. I literally dance every morning before work at five and after I get home. My prayer life continues to grow by leaps and bounds as I gain more understanding about God's unfailing love and faithfulness through reading his word.

As I continue on this journey called life, I am calm and content since God is in control. For sure, there will be good days and bad, but I have put my faith and trust in him, knowing that all things are done for my good and his glory. When I decided to tell my story, I set a goal to end the book at the two-year anniversary of Shirl's death. So I have now come to the end of my personal story regarding my devastating losses that led to my spiritual awakening. Though that part of my life is over, I continue my lifelong journey with the Lord Jesus. Since I now have a complete understanding that my life is totally under God's control, not mine. I exist to complete his will for my life, which is to walk in his ways, to praise and glorify all that he is, and to thank him for all the blessings he has given me. Not all my days are rosy but I have a lot to be thankful for, and my faith continues to grow. I know that the Lord walks with me and comforts me. This earth is only my temporary home as *I am not of this world*. I also know he will help me get through whatever trials are ahead of me for he has promised to never abandon me. I live contentedly and have no worries or fears, believing in the hope that his unfailing love and faithfulness will be with me all the days of my life. I am sure of one thing, I am looking forward to the day when I meet the Lord my God and hope to hear, "Well done, my good and faithful servant."

My Lasting Message of Hope

In closing, I have to tell you that the title of the book really came to fruition, *The Gray Seed (Bible) Became a Peace Lily.*

If you truly want to find purpose, passion, and complete inner joy in your life, try getting to know the Lord, our God, through a personal relationship with Jesus Christ. He is the way, the truth, and the life. I urge you to get a Bible and start reading God's word. I assure you that you won't regret it and you'll never look back.

My hope is that anyone who reads this will be encouraged by my testimony and start a new lifelong journey with the Lord. May God bless all of you. *Thanks be to God!*

About the Author

Karen is the fifth of six children (1 brother and 4 sisters). Her parents and three of her sisters are now deceased. She was raised in Northampton Ma. and attended area grade schools. In 1975 she became the first girl to enter the all-boys trades shop program at Smith Vocational High School after she and her father fought with the school board. Karen went through carpentry, auto mechanics, auto body, agriculture, and electrical and chose the electrical shop as her final selection. She graduated with top honors from the electrical department. In her senior year she was approached by the International Brotherhood of Electrical Workers to enroll in their apprenticeship program. There was a test to get in. Karen decided to try it and came in second. She also received scholarships to college and then had to decide whether to go to school or work. She chose the union. Karen started the four-year program but after only two years she took the license exam and became one of the first women in Ma. to become a licensed electrician. Karen worked as a union electrician for five years. She then had a call from her high school guidance counselor who said Digital Equipment Corp was looking for an electrician, so he gave them her name. Karen went to work for them from 1984 to 1991 as she had a career ending injury. After her recovery she went to work as a manufacturing employee making various cutting tools. Karen became a production supervisor and left in 2001 due to company downsizing. Karen then landed her present job in 2002 as a Section 8 low income housing inspector where she still works today. She is very lucky to be in a job she feels she was meant for (her calling). Karen loves animals and has a home in Easthampton Ma. where she lives with her spouse Shirl since 2001, even though she is now deceased. Karen has two talking parrots, three cats and fish that keep her busy. She is also very involved with her church E.C.C as a volunteer. She also does grocery shopping for homebound seniors through the Easthampton senior service center. Her personal life is otherwise quiet, but she is very happy and at peace due to her very personal relationship with God. Karen now let's God lead her where he wants her to go thus her yoke has been easy and her burden light. Thanks to all of you.

Epilogue

In the 4 years, since I finished the last chapter of this book, many new chapters have opened. I have continued to grow in my Faith as I walk with my Lord Jesus Christ. I have heard many people say they want to know what God's will is for their life, I have also asked this question while I continue to gain a deeper understanding of "Who my God is". The truth I am discovering through the Lord's word is that he wants me to fully surrender to his will, following and trusting him in everything even when the path seems ridiculous. For instance, the 2nd release of this book. I have been contacted by numerous publishers to which I told them the book is finished. So, I figured that was it whether the book sold or not I had completed my mission to give my testimony about what happened to me. So, that my path to healing might encourage others who are going through difficult times and how the Lord, has helped me get through all of it. Not, as my lord by the holy spirit has prompted me to do it. My response was yes Lord thy will be done.

I know, that my 'Lord wants what's best for me' and he will always provide for my needs. I know, many people say that the Lord doesn't always answer prayers but I have, learned from all my experiences that he answers every single prayer. Sometimes, it's not the answer we want to receive but, if we keep following him and trusting in him that he knows the best way for this life. Where this is his life lived through me and he will make sure that I get exactly where I'm supposed to according to his will. On, his timetable for his purpose and his glory. Amen to my 'God in the name of the Lord Jesus Christ' and the Holy Spirit forever and ever. I know there is, but one God through one Faith by one baptism. I now understand the meaning when my God said when they ask my name you tell them

"IAM that IAM." God says I am your savior, provider, comforter, healer best friend, and everything you need. I am at peace with my Lord safe and secure knowing that he loves me beyond all measure and will never abandon me or forsake me.

I love the Lord, with all my heart and soul and am determined to walk with him in this life while praising, worshipping, and thanking him for all the blessings every single day. As I walk with my Lord, each day I find a blessing no matter where I am or what my circumstances such as a beautiful sunrise or sunset or a colorful bird that crosses my path or a deer or rabbit, everything good comes from the Lord and I thank him continually for the blessings. I am at the same job, now over 20 years. I still have, Alex and Ember but also have a new addition to my parrot family a female African grey, which I agreed to take in because a friend who had cancer and has now passed on knew I had parrots. He asked if I would take his bird if something happened to him to which I said absolutely. Her name is Chloe and she or should I say we all have adjusted well.

Overall, things are going well. I'm not going to lie to you it has been a difficult road and yes taken me almost 7 years to fully know the depth of his healing Love. I tell you, that I am dedicated to serving my Lord's purpose for his glory by taking time for Bible scripture reading, praising, and praying every day. I can say openly and honestly, that I love the Lord with all my heart and soul. And when I think about him, talk to him, or when I pray to him my emotions always come to the surface through, overwhelming tears of joy and gratitude as I never knew I could be so loved and that I could have an intimate relationship with 'God Almighty'. So, that when I spend time with him it takes my breath away and I can't get enough of his word. My hope, and prayer for everyone is that you seek the lord and get into a deep intimate relationship with the "Lord God almighty in the name of Jesus Christ". May God bless you and keep you safe, healthy, and rich in spirit all the days of your life as I am Amen.

www.ingramcontent.com/pod-product-compliance
Lightning Source LLC
LaVergne TN
LVHW010618070526
838199LV00063BA/5190